Masseur & Massage Therapist

Earning $50,000–$100,000 with a High School Diploma or Less

Announcer

Car Mechanic

Chef

Cosmetologist

DJ

Dog Groomer

Energizing Energy Markets:
Clean Coal, Shale, Oil, Wind, and Solar

Farming, Ranching, and Agriculture

Masseur & Massage Therapist

Personal Assistant

Presenting Yourself: Business Manners,
Personality, and Etiquette

Referee

The Arts: Dance, Music, Theater, and Fine Art

Truck Driver

Earning $50,000–$100,000
with a High School Diploma or Less

Masseur &
Massage Therapist

CONNOR SYREWICZ

MASON CREST

Clinton Macomb
Public Library

Mason Crest
450 Parkway Drive, Suite D
Broomall, PA 19008
www.masoncrest.com

Printed in the United States of America.

First printing
9 8 7 6 5 4 3 2 1

Series ISBN: 978-1-4222-2886-9
ISBN: 978-1-4222-2896-8
ebook ISBN: 978-1-4222-8932-7

The Library of Congress has cataloged the
        hardcopy format(s) as follows:

                Library of Congress Cataloging-in-Publication Data

Syrewicz, Connor.
  Masseur & massage therapist / Connor Syrewicz.
      pages cm. – (Earning $50,000 - $100,000 with a high school diploma or less)
  Includes bibliographical references and index.
      ISBN 978-1-4222-2896-8 (hardcover) – ISBN 978-1-4222-2886-9 (series) –
ISBN 978-1-4222-8932-7 (ebook)
  1. Massage therapy–Juvenile literature. 2. Massage therapy–Vocational guidance–Juvenile literature. 3. Masseurs–Juvenile literature. I. Title. II. Title: Masseur and massage therapist.
  RM722.S97 2014
  615.8'22–dc23
                                2013015568

Produced by Vestal Creative Services.
www.vestalcreative.com

Contents

CHAPTER 1

Careers Without College

nyone who has ever had a sore back can tell you how wonderful a massage feels. Massages can be very relaxing, but that is far from their only purpose. Some people need massages for medical reasons. One form of massage therapy can help heal a serious injury, while other types of massage can relieve stress. "It's a profession in which I can help people," Karen Spoolman explains. "Being a massage therapist is rewarding to me because I know I'm helping people. I'm making a real difference in their lives."

A massage therapist is someone who uses physical touch to manipulate the soft muscles under the skin. Common areas to have massaged are the back, neck, shoulders, and legs. You may have heard someone talk

Craniosacral therapy is a very specific massage technique that involves light touches on the bones of the skull (including the face and mouth), spine, and pelvis to release tension and improve body movement.

about a torn, pulled, or sore muscle. An experienced massage therapist can help fix all these problems through multiple sessions of **therapy**. Massage therapists can be found in many places including **spas**, hospitals, doctor offices, or fitness centers.

Some massage therapists use only their hands while others might also use their elbows and feet. Heat, lotion, or oil may be used to make the massage even more effective. How each client is treated depends entirely on why he or she is getting the massage. As a **licensed** massage therapist with about twelve years of experience, Karen has learned plenty of different massage techniques. "The way you treat a sports injury is different from how you would treat an elderly patient with back problems," Karen explains. "A good massage therapist needs to know the difference or someone can get hurt."

Although all massage therapists should know a little bit about every type of massage, some choose to specialize in a certain area. Karen, for example, is a **rehabilitative** massage therapist. She mostly works with patients who need massage therapy to help repair injuries. For example, a person who has been in a car crash might have whiplash, a muscular injury in the neck—and a special type of massage therapy will help this injury repair and feel better over time.

Looking at the Words

Therapy is treatment intended to relieve or heal a disorder.

Spas are places offering beauty and health treatments such as steam baths, exercise, and massages.

Licensed means officially allowed to practice.

Rehabilitative means helping to restore to good condition.

The ancient Egyptians used hand and foot massages to promote health.

Masseurs and Massage Therapists

In the past, if you told someone you were visiting a massage therapist, masseur (male), or masseuse (female), it would have meant the same thing. Today, the terms are a little different. While a massage therapist is licensed and trained, a masseur or masseuse does not need to be. In addition to being paid a lot more, a licensed massage therapist is also more knowledgeable about the human body. If you have an injury or other stress-related problem, a massage therapist will be better at helping you. If you are only looking to get a massage for relaxation purposes, an unlicensed masseur or masseuse is an acceptable alternative, although an untrained masseur or masseuse may not do a very good job. Some licensed massage therapists still use the traditional name of masseur or masseuse, which can be very confusing! If you ever have any questions, be sure to ask before therapy begins. A licensed massage therapist will be happy to show you his or her license.

An Evolving Career

Muscle pain has existed for as long as humans have, so massage therapy has actually been around for thousands of years. In fact, massage

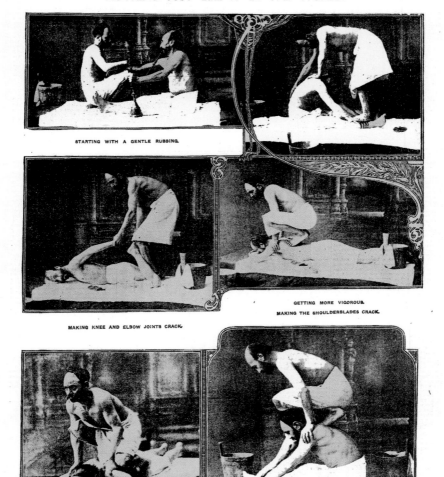

New-York Tribune.

PART II.   SUNDAY, DECEMBER 17, 1905.   EIGHT PAGES.

AT A PUBLIC BATH IN TIFLIS—WITH THE REAL THING IN MASSAGE—
NOTHING JUST LIKE IT IN THE WORLD.

STARTING WITH A GENTLE RUBBING.

MAKING KNEE AND ELBOW JOINTS CRACK.

GETTING MORE VIGOROUS.
MAKING THE SHOULDERBLADES CRACK.

This 1905 newspaper demonstrates several massage techniques, and proclaims that there's "nothing just like it in the world."

therapy is one of the earliest forms of **noninvasive** medicine. "Many early cultures believed that massages using herbs and oils could ease pain and help with relaxation," Karen explains. Today, we know massage therapy does both those things.

Muscles can be very complex. Because a massage therapist cannot directly see how a massage affects the muscles, he or she must rely completely on the patient's feedback. "I'm not a doctor," Karen says, "but I do sometimes feel like one. I have to be pretty thorough with what I know about a patient. I ask a lot of questions and I take a lot of notes. By taking a patient's history and discussing what he or she wants out of therapy, we can both decide what type of therapy is best."

Some of the first people to perform a type of massage therapy were doctors. In the 1800s, doctors began to recognize that massage therapy helped a patient heal after an injury. Many injured patients were told to use some form of massage therapy in addition to other forms of physical therapy.

It wasn't until the 1900s that massage therapy became respected as its own field. Schools began to open that trained massage therapists in how to perform massages effectively and safely. Today, there are tests that a massage therapist must pass in order to become licensed. "The test isn't easy," Karen explains. "It makes sense that it wouldn't be, really, if you think about it. After all, you'll be working on living human beings. You need to be able to prove you're capable of doing the job, that you won't hurt people instead of help them."

Each year, new techniques in massage therapy are being designed and discussed. "The human body is a very interesting thing," Karen

Resort spas, where everything is designed to create an atmosphere of relaxation and peace, offer massage therapists some of the highest-paying jobs in the industry.

says. "Even though we know so much about it, there's always more to learn. Over the years, we've learned that some forms of therapy work better than others. So massage therapy is always improving."

The College Question

"When I graduated from high school," says Karen, "I wasn't sure what I wanted to be. I decided to wait to go to college." For a student who already knows exactly what he or she wants to do in life, college might be the right decision. However, college can be very expensive, and if you don't know which degree you want to pursue, it can feel like a waste of money.

After a few years of working at a doctor's office as an administrative assistant, Karen realized her passion. "I first got interested in massage therapy when I met people who came to our office with sore muscles," she says. "A lot of time, the doctor I worked for would refer them to a massage therapist."

Although Karen had heard about spas and relaxation therapy, she had never before realized all the benefits of massage therapy as a job choice. "When I began looking into being a massage therapist, I was surprised when I realized I didn't need to go to college. Instead, I just needed to go through a training program."

Some massage therapists still choose to go to college, but it is not a requirement. For people like Karen, jumping right into a training program might be the best option.

Rob Carlos has only recently started out in the massage industry. "I'm glad I chose to become a message therapist," Rob says. "Finding a job was very easy for me. Plus, I don't have to worry about any student loans." Unlike Rob, some of his friends have had a hard time finding a job.

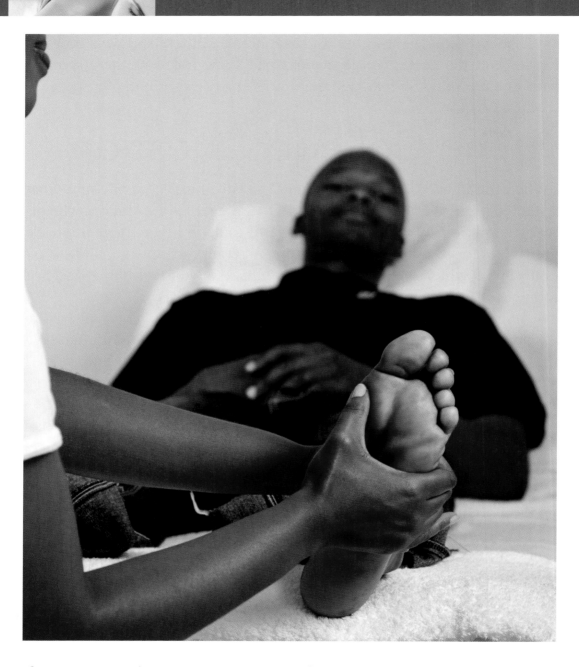

If you want to become a massage therapist, you need to be comfortable handling people's bodies, including their feet.

Masseur & Massage Therapist

"I knew I wanted to become a massage therapist from the moment I started seeing a massage therapist myself," Rob recalls. "I was even more excited when I learned the training was something I could afford. My folks don't have a lot of money, and I hated the idea of going into debt."

Although many high school graduates choose to pursue a college education, some of them will have difficulty finding a job after they graduate. Because college can be very expensive, many students are forced to take out loans to afford it. If they can't find a job after college, they will have a hard time paying back those loans, which leads to even more problems. By taking a course in massage therapy, Rob was able to afford the costs without borrowing money.

By working hard and pursuing their dreams, both Rob and Karen now have careers they truly enjoy. "Today," Karen says, "the same doctor's office I once worked for now refers patients to me."

CHAPTER 2

What Do Masseurs & Massage Therapists Do?

When you have a broken bone, you might see a bone doctor. If you have a toothache, you might see a dentist. When it comes to muscle pain, a massage therapist may be the best person to help you. Sometimes, people choose to go to a massage therapist in order to relieve stress or anxiety. Others go to a massage therapist to help an injury heal. Because a massage therapist's job is as complex as the clients he sees, not every massage therapist is the same.

Ashiatsu is a type of massage therapy in which the therapist walks on the client's back, using bars and other props for support to vary pressure and weight.

"Being a massage therapist is much more than simply giving massages," Paul Goldstein says. With almost thirty-two years in the profession, Paul is extremely experienced in both relaxation and rehabilitative massage therapy. "Part of the job is giving massages," he says, "but there is so much more that goes into it."

First, a massage therapist must get to know a client. A massage therapist might ask about a client's medical history or what he or she wants to get out of massage therapy.

A massage therapist also has plenty of tools at his disposal. These might include massage tables, chairs, lights, heat lamps, stones, oils, and lotions. Paul adds, "But the most important tool is myself." Because massages are often given with the hands, elbows, or even feet, a massage therapist's body can be used as a tool in many ways. That's why it's important that Paul keeps his body in shape. It takes strength and **flexibility** to be a good massage therapist.

After deciding on which type of massage therapy the patient or client needs, the massage therapist gets to work. "Depending on the type of massage therapy, we may or may not communicate during the massage," Paul says. "Some people like to talk the whole time I'm working on them. Other people zone out and don't want me to interrupt their relaxation."

If an area is especially rough or tense, a massage therapist might tell the client and spend a little bit more time on this area. A massage can be as short as five minutes or take longer than an hour. "It all depends on what the client wants and pays for," Paul explains.

"Even after the massage, my job is far from done," he adds. In order to help a client take better care of his or her body, a massage therapist

A relaxing environment is important to many kinds of massage therapy. This spa offers outdoor massages.

may give suggestions. "I advise some clients on how to have a better posture while sitting or standing. I also give suggestions on how to stay relaxed at home. If a person in involved in sports, I might teach them special stretches or strengthening exercises."

Even after taking a patient's history, performing the massage, and giving advice, a massage therapist's job is still not over. If he works in a salon or spa, he may have other responsibilities, such as cleaning his work area between clients. Ever since he started working on his own, Paul must take appointments and do his own paperwork. "It's tiring, and I don't get paid for it, but it's all part of the job."

Atmosphere

Depending on which type of massage therapy you get, the atmosphere can differ. Relaxation massage therapists might try to create a calming environment by using dim lights, candles, incense, scented oils, and soft, soothing music. A rehabilitative massage therapist is more likely to give massages in a bright room with more than one client present. However, all massage therapists are different. Finding the right massage therapist for you is a very important part of the experience. Be sure to ask a lot of questions while booking your first appointment.

Relaxation Specialists

"If you're tense from a hard day at work or you're going through a bad time in your life, I highly recommend seeing a massage therapist who specializes in relaxation," Paul says. "A good massage can be a great reliever of stress. Your mind and your body are connected—so if your body relaxes, your mind will feel better too. You'll have more emotional energy."

A person who works in a physically demanding career might also need the occasional massage to keep his or her muscles from becoming too sore on the job. A relaxation therapist can typically be found at a spa, mall, hotel, or private practice.

Paul spent the first five years of his career working at several different spas. "Each place is different," Paul says. "The environment, the

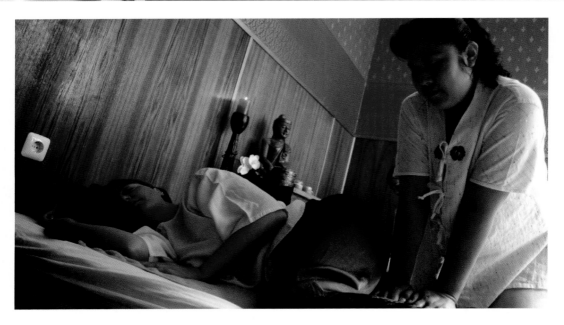

This woman is receiving a Thai massage at a spa.

type of massages offered, the availability, and the price can all vary." The typical massage can cost anywhere from $50 to $100.

Along with the many reasons to see a massage therapist, there are also different types of massage therapy. No two bodies are the same, and finding the right type of massage therapy can take a little while. "I suggest speaking directly with a massage therapist," Paul advises. "Discuss what you want out of massage therapy—and then the massage therapist will do his best to try to find the best type of massage for you." Many people try several different types of massage before finding a favorite.

"The most common type of massage therapy in the United States is Swedish massage therapy," Paul says. Chances are, when you think of what a massage is, you may be thinking of this type. It is somewhat gentle and can involve lotions and oils. A massage therapist delivers this type of massage by kneading the muscles and rubbing in circular motions with his hands.

Not every massage just uses the hands, though. Some massages also use other body parts or tools to help the client feel even more relaxed. One example of an extremely relaxing type of massage therapy is an aromatherapy massage. In addition to a physical massage, scented oils are also used to help relieve stress. A stone massage uses stones that are heated to sooth the body and loosen tight muscles.

Some massages differ based on where or how the body is touched. During a shiatsu massage, a massage therapist will use his or her fingers to press down at certain points to relieve tension. "Certain massages are more active than others," Paul explains. "A Thai massage is similar to yoga, except the massage therapist is the one to move and stretch you into different positions. You don't have to do a thing."

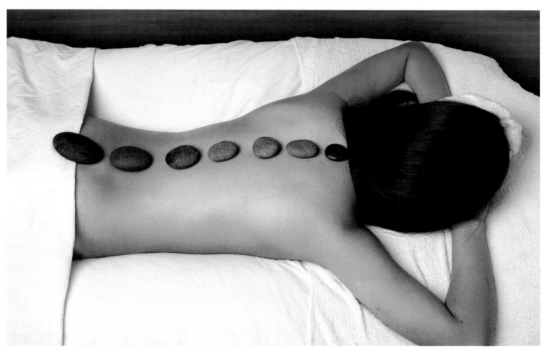

The premise behind hot-stone massage therapy is that the direct heat of the stones relaxes muscles, allowing the therapist access to deeper muscle layers.

Massage can relieve older people's muscle pains and improve their circulation and flexibility.

There are also a few types of massages for people in special situations. A pregnant woman, for example, might want to get a pregnancy massage. Unlike other massages, a pregnancy massage is mindful of the growing baby inside the mother's womb. Instead of lying flat on a table, a woman will be positioned in such a way that is comfortable for her. Pregnancy can lead to back pain and other muscular distress, and a pregnancy massage is meant to ease stress, reduce swelling, and help with the pain associated with pregnancy. There are special massages designed for the elderly as well.

Rehabilitative Massage Therapists

Unlike relaxation massage therapists, where anyone can make an appointment, patients are almost always referred by a doctor to rehabilitative massage therapy. When a person is injured, she may need to have physical therapy. In order for an injury to completely heal, a client may need to visit more than one type of physical therapist. Massage therapy is just one form of physical therapy.

Some rehabilitative massage therapists work at a chiropractor's office, which is where Paul works now. A **chiropractor** helps realign and examine bones in the back and neck. "But," explains Paul, "a chiropractor doesn't do much for soft-tissue muscles. That's where I come in." As a team, a chiropractor and a massage therapist can work together to repair an injury over time.

Looking at the Words

A **chiropractor** is a medical practitioner who physically adjusts the spine.

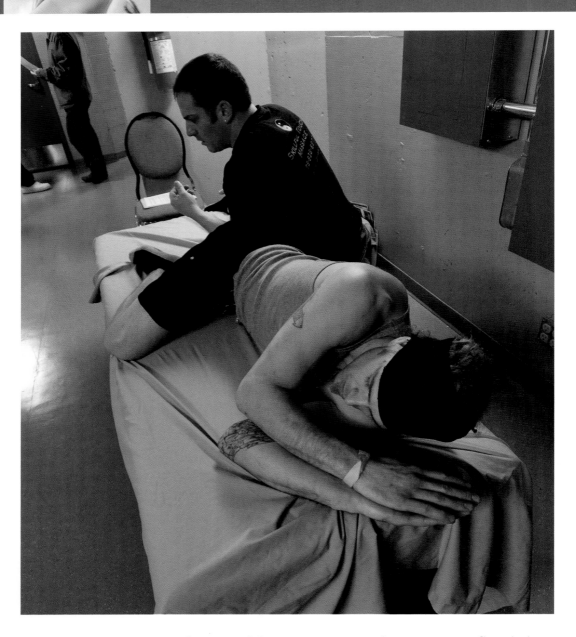

Sports massages relieve athletes' pain and improves flexibility. This massage therapist works with boxers before and after their fights.

MASSEUR & MASSAGE THERAPIST

In addition to helping an injury heal, rehabilitative massage therapy is different in other ways. "I find that I communicate with a patient a lot more during a rehabilitative massage than I did when I was giving a relaxation massage, Paul explains. "In order for me to know how to treat an injury in just the right way, I need to talk to the client directly while a massage is happening. I will ask what feels good or bad. This way, I can know exactly how the patient is feeling and make sure I am doing a good job." Because injured muscles can be delicate, obtaining feedback from a client also prevents Paul from making the injury worse.

Like relaxation massage therapy, rehabilitative therapy will use special types of massage. "A deep-tissue massage is a bit rougher than a normal massage because it is designed to target the deepest layers of muscle," Paul explains. A person receiving this type of massage often feels a little sore for a day or two afterward. Because of the nature of the massage, this is completely normal and to be expected. In addition to loosening your muscles, deep-tissue massages can help you recover from an injury faster.

Someone who plays a sport or is injured while playing a sport needs a sports massage. How the muscle is treated depends partly on the sport being played. Some sports require more strength, while others require more flexibility. Sports massages can help keep athletes' muscles working at their best.

"It's a satisfying career," Paul says. "I've been doing it for years now, and I still love it."

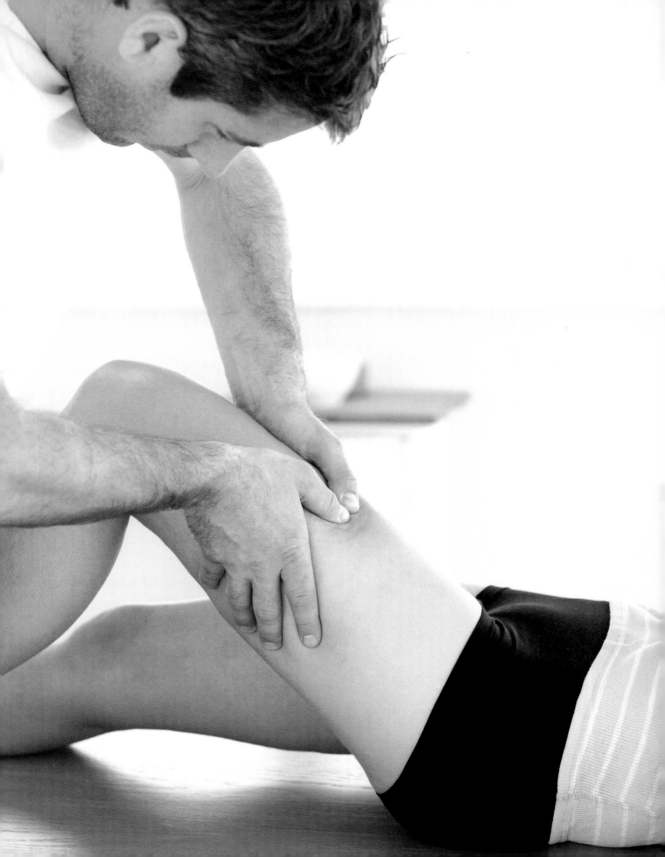

CHAPTER 3

How Can I Become a Masseur or Massage Therapist?

Becoming a massage therapist takes some time and a lot of hard work—but there are a few different paths to consider taking.

Getting Trained

Although the amount of training you need depends on which state you are in, it's not uncommon for a massage therapist to

Human anatomy

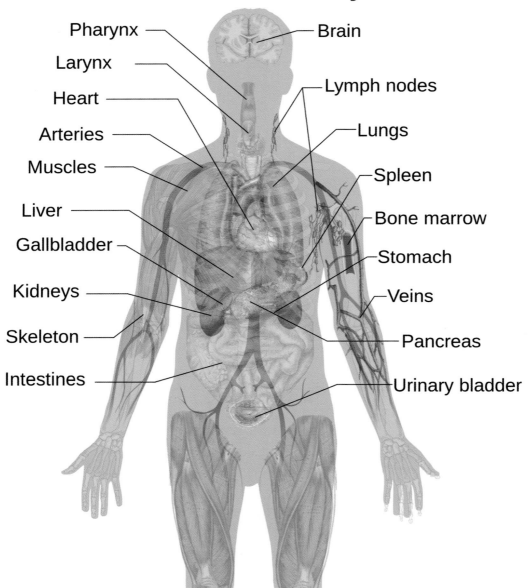

Pharynx — Brain

Larynx

Heart — Lymph nodes

Arteries — Lungs

Muscles — Spleen

Liver — Bone marrow

Gallbladder — Stomach

Kidneys — Veins

Skeleton — Pancreas

Intestines — Urinary bladder

A massage therapist needs to understand human anatomy, including the placement of major organs.

need between 500 and 1,000 hours of experience. "At first, I thought it would be easy," Karen Spoolman says. "Boy, was I wrong! Training really felt like a full-time job."

In addition to pursuing her 500 hours of training, Karen worked a full-time job to be able to afford the training, which can cost over $5,000. "Luckily, the doctor's office I worked for was pretty accommodating. The doctor was supportive and understood when I needed to go to a class. Of course, I needed to make up my hours. I got pretty tired fitting in everything I had to do. I didn't have much free time for a while."

"Even though you don't need to go to college, you still need an education," Karen explains. Massage therapists have to learn how to safely and effectively give a good massage. Usually, the only requirement for starting a program in massage therapy is a high school diploma.

"You learn a lot in training," Karen says. "I was mostly taught about the human **anatomy** and how the body moves." She was also given hands-on training by an experienced massage therapist. "I learned how to use different massage techniques and solve problems. Like if a patient had a stubborn back pain, maybe I needed to talk to him about his feet and his shoes. Things like that, where different parts of the body are connected. You can experience pain in one part of your body that's actually caused by a problem somewhere else." Good massage therapists encounter all sorts of situations and must be good problem-solvers as a result.

Even though there was a lot to learn in the classroom, there was an equal amount for Karen to learn on her own. A massage therapist will be working with clients constantly, so she will need to know how to speak

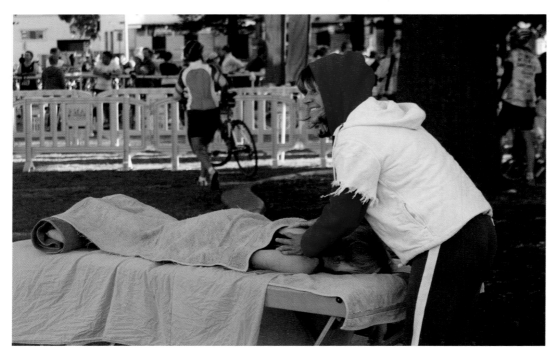

Sometimes massage therapists take their skills where they're most needed. This masseuse is offering massages to runners in a triathalon.

to people. "Because I had already worked at a doctor's office, I spoke with people on a regular basis, but I still felt a little shy," Karen says. "I was a really quiet kid in high school. Being a massage therapist was new to me and I wasn't sure how I should speak to patients."

In order to feel more comfortable in her new job, Karen decided to visit a massage therapist herself. "I went for a few sessions and paid attention to how she spoke to me. I noticed the kinds of questions she asked and her tone of voice. I told her I was in training, so she gave me a lot of advice." By seeing a massage therapist in action, Karen was able to better understand how she should be acting. No matter which occupation you choose, observation is always very important. Before you have

experience of your own, it's always a good idea to learn from watching those who do.

At the end of training, a massage therapist may be required to take any number of exams, depending on the state where he or she wants to be licensed. These exams can cost a few hundred dollars; they vary, based on what type of massage therapist you would like to become.

After two years of training, all Karen's hard work paid off. "By the time I graduated as a licensed massage therapist, I was ready to work in a career I'd fallen in love with."

Deciding to Become a Massage Therapist

For Justin Harns, a massage therapist with twelve years of experience, becoming a massage therapist was a very personal choice. "When I was a teenager, I broke my ankle and couldn't walk on it for several months while it was in a cast. After the cast was taken off, I needed to go to a physical therapist to strengthen the muscles that hadn't been used." Part of Justin's physical therapy was seeing a massage therapist. From that point on, Justin knew what he wanted to be when he grew up. "I wanted to help other injured people get better," he says.

Justin started preparing to be a massage therapist while he was still in high school. He took every biology class he could to learn about the human anatomy. He practiced giving his friends and family massages.

Once Justin finally graduated, he immediately signed up for a training program to help him become a massage therapist. "In order to afford the classes, I had a part-time job at a gym which worked out well for me. I was able to learn even more about the human body while working."

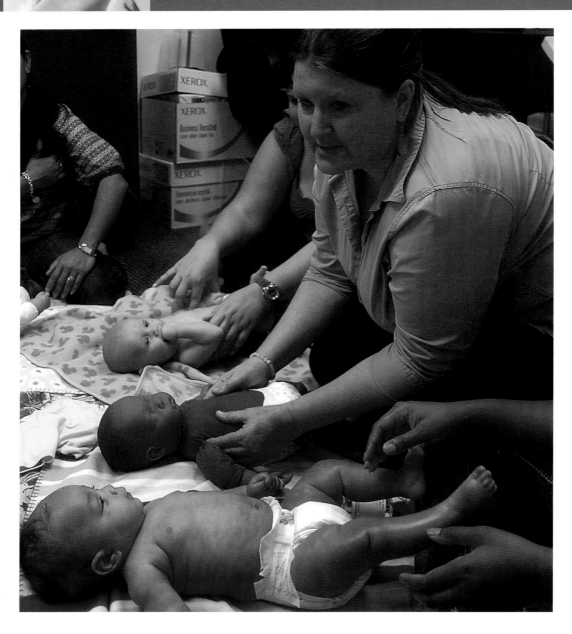

Even babies can benefit from a massage! This massage therapist is using a doll to demonstrate techniques to new mothers.

At the age of twenty, Justin completed training. Finding a job was easy for him because the field of massage therapy was growing at a fast rate. "I originally worked at a fitness center. I enjoyed my job, but I wasn't paid as well as I would have liked. In order to earn the kind of pay I wanted to have, I would need to be more experienced." Working at the fitness center allowed Justin to gain that experience.

Looking at the Words

Self-employed means working for oneself instead of for a company.

Modalities are types, kinds, or methods.

Where Do You Go Next?

Justin knows what it's like to slowly work your way up to the top. "I recommend reading as much as you can about new techniques, new research. Don't just settle for staying at the same level year after year. And ask other massage therapists for advice. We can learn a lot from each other."

There is a lot of money to be made within the industry, but the trick is finding your niche. While most massage therapists are **self-employed**, many others work for spas, chiropractors, and fitness centers. Some massage therapists even work in malls or hotels. Each area of employment has its own environment and specialty. Spas, malls, and hotels usually offer relaxation massage, while chiropractors and fitness centers might help with sports injuries or work-related muscle problems.

Although a massage therapist must learn the basics of each type of massage, he or she may choose a specialty while still in school. With almost fifty different **modalities**, there will always be a lot to learn. Even after school, a massage therapist might continue taking classes to learn

new techniques. "The difference between a good massage therapist and a great massage therapist is how willing they are to learn something new," Justin says.

Modalities

What do you imagine when you think of a massage? The truth is not all massages are the same. In fact, some types of massage don't even involve the massage therapist physically touching the body at all! Massages are sometimes named after their place of origin. For example, a Swedish massage was developed in Sweden and involves rubbing the body with long strokes. A stone massage is named after the stones that are used to rub against the body, which may be heated or cooled to enhance the experience. Depending on whom you ask, there are almost fifty different types, or modalities of massage. If you ever go to a massage therapist, be sure to ask which modalities he or she is trained in. You may be advised to find a therapist that can perform a specific modality for your needs.

Is Massage Therapy Right for Me?

"Before you pursue a career in massage therapy, you should know what you are getting yourself into," Justin says. "It can be a very exciting

career for the right person, but not everyone will like it. You have to be comfortable touching people's bodies."

Massage therapists almost always take patients by appointment, which can make their schedules very flexible.

At the same time, a massage therapist must stick to the commitments he or she makes. "I rarely take sick days," Justin explains. "People are relying on me and I don't want to let them down."

About half of the massage therapists in the United States are self-employed, which means they run their own business. As a self-employed massage therapist, Justin understands the need for **self-discipline**. Seeing clients is just a fraction of Justin's job. "At first, it was hard to find my own clients, but I'm glad I work for myself now. I don't need to pay anyone to work for me, and I have more freedom. But it also means I need to book the appointments and follow up on them myself." Justin alone does all of the paperwork and scheduling.

Being a massage therapist is a very hands-on job, which requires any massage therapist to be completely comfortable with the idea of touching another person. "While I was first going through training," Jason remembers, "it felt very awkward touching a stranger's back, let alone his thighs or feet. I had given my friends massages for years, but I didn't realize it would feel different with someone I didn't know. People come in all shapes and sizes. Their skin feels different. They smell different. At first, it can kind of bother you. After a while, though, you get used to it. It just feels normal." For some people, the initial awkwardness goes away. For others, it might not. Keep this in mind when thinking about pursuing this career.

This career is also hard work. "Massage therapy can be pretty taxing on my body," Justin admits. "Even though I am helping other people relax, I am not relaxing on the job. I'm working hard. It's hard, manual labor." It is also not uncommon for massage therapists to spend a lot of time on their feet while performing a massage. After eight hours of working on your feet, you'll be tired! In Justin's case, he feels his mind gets a good workout, too. "I need to stay focused. The client is paying me to do a good job and I don't want to give anything but my best."

Although Justin might worry most about the people on his table, he needs to take care of himself, too. "If I don't use my hands in just the right way, I could injure myself. Not only will that physically hurt, but it could put me out of work for weeks. I get a little paranoid about taking care of my hands. If my hands don't work, I don't have a job." While a massage therapist is still training, he will be given advice on how to prevent self-injury by using proper techniques.

In order to compensate for the physical and mental stress he endures on his job, Justin visits his own massage therapist once a week. "It gives me a chance to relax and loosen my muscles. I don't know what I would do if I couldn't fit it into my schedule." Although it can be stressful, Justin truly enjoys his job. "I am doing something I enjoy. I have never doubted for a second that this is the right career for me."

What All Massage Therapists Need

"When working as a massage therapist," Justin advises, "there are really two important skills you must have. In addition to being trained to do the physical aspect of the job, you must also know how to talk to people." A lot of the time, a person who visits a massage therapist has a very personal story behind why he or she needs to be there in the first place. The patient may wish to confide this to a massage therapist, which

can turn massage therapy into a very personal experience.

A good massage therapist will also have other emotional and mental skills as well. The Bureau of Labor Statistics lists five important qualities that every massage therapist should have.

- **Communication skills.** Massage therapists need to listen carefully to clients to understand what they want to achieve through massage appointments.
- **Decision-making skills.** Massage therapists must evaluate each client's needs and recommend the best treatment based on that person's needs.
- **Empathy.** Massage therapists must give clients a positive experience, which requires building trust between therapist and client. Making clients feel comfortable is necessary for therapists to expand their client base.
- **Physical stamina.** Massage therapists may give several treatments during a workday and have to stay on their feet throughout massage appointments.
- **Physical strength and dexterity.** Massage therapists must be strong and able to exert pressure through a variety of movements of the arms and hands when manipulating a client's muscles.

Although not listed, another important quality a massage therapist should have is the desire to keep learning. A massage therapist might

Being a massage therapist will give you many opportunities to make a difference in the world by improving others' quality of life. These therapists are donating their time to give free massages to emergency relief workers after a hurricane.

try to become trained in new modalities, for example, or learn different types of massage. The more specialties a massage therapist knows, the better equipped he or she will be at fulfilling the needs of patients.

"Massage therapy is constantly changing," Justin says. "I am always learning something new. Plus, there is a lot I still don't know even though I've worked in the field this long." In his spare time, Justin attends classes to learn the newest developments in massage therapy.

"And it's not just about how much you know," Justin adds. "Social skills are also important. If I didn't know how to talk to clients, they probably wouldn't want to come back." The most successful massage therapists are often very friendly with their clients. "If we get along, it makes the whole experience much more enjoyable for everyone involved. People tell me amazing things. I consider it an honor that they trust me enough to share their lives with me. And it keeps my job from ever getting boring!"

CHAPTER 4

How Much Can I Make?

Until a massage therapist has worked in the field for a number of years, she might have to deal with a low salary. A really good massage therapist can eventually earn over $50,000, but getting to this point can take some time.

"I moved from job to job for a while. I worked at a spa for a year and then a chiropractor's office for three," Justin Harns says. "At the same time, I was going to classes to be trained in other modalities of massage. I wanted to learn everything!"

At the age of twenty-six, Justin decided to start his own business as a rehabilitative massage therapist. "At first, my business was very small because I didn't have many clients of my own. I set up a special room in my own house for massage therapy. It was connected to the side door and looked like an office. I made sure it looked completely professional but having it in my house kept it affordable for me."

A massage therapist can gain clients in a number of ways—and the more clients he has, the more money he will make. The Internet is a great resource for letting people know what you have to offer. Potential clients can find Justin's information online and contact him directly. He also advertises using a personal website. Doctor offices and physical therapists may also refer people in need to him.

As Justin becomes more popular, he gains more clients. "The number of clients I have has grown slowly. After about two years of working out of my house, I was making enough that I could rent a space in an office building. Now I really felt like a professional!" Justin still owns a private practice and prefers it that way. "I like the freedom and the pay," he says. "I wouldn't trade this job for the world."

The price of a one-hour massage can range anywhere from $50 to over $100, depending on the reputation and experience of the massage therapist. How much a massage therapist actually makes, though, depends on several factors. The first, and most important, is experience. A massage therapist who has just graduated cannot make as much as someone with over twenty years of experience. "Climbing from the bottom to the top takes time—but it's possible," Andrea Fogel says. With more than ten years in the industry, Andrea is finally earning just over $50,000 a year.

"You increase your chances of doing well," she says, "if you're careful about where you work." A massage therapist working in a wealthy or densely populated area will probably make more money than a person working in an area with a low population. Certain settings allow you

to charge more as well. "For example," Andrea explains, "a relaxation massage therapist in a five-star hotel or resort will make a better salary than a massage therapist working at a cheaper hotel."

Only about one in four massage therapists work full time. In the United States, a person who works full time spends at least forty or more hours working each week. For a massage therapist, work hours include much more than just giving massages. A massage therapist needs to prepare, order materials, and make appointments, among other tasks. But if she's self-employed, she doesn't get paid for doing these necessary tasks. This means she might work forty hours a week—but only get paid for twenty or thirty.

Although some massage therapists might enjoy working part time, it is not always a choice. "Most massage therapists work almost entirely by appointment," Andrea says. "If I don't receive a lot of appointments during one week, then I simply don't work as much." The less Andrea works, the less money she makes.

Tips

Whether or not it is appropriate to tip a massage therapist depends entirely on the type of massage you are receiving. It is customary to leave at least a fifteen percent tip after receiving a relaxation massage at a spa or hotel. If you truly enjoyed the massage, an even bigger tip is a nice way to say, "Job well done." However, if you are receiving a massage for medical reasons, it is not appropriate to tip. Instead, you can say thank you by referring other people to that practice. If you aren't sure of whether or not you should tip, don't be afraid to ask! It is not an uncommon or embarrassing question.

One way for a massage therapist to make more money is by owning his or her own business. If you work for someone else, you will not receive all of the money from a massage. For example, if a massage costs $50, you will only receive a small portion of that. The rest goes to the business owner. In comparison, when you work for yourself, you receive 100 percent of the money. Of course, this doesn't mean you won't also have extra costs as a self-employed massage therapist. You'll have to pay for your office space and the tools you use. And you may have a lot more headaches as well if you're running your own business! On the other hand, you'll have more freedom to work when and where you want.

Considering all these factors, pay for a massage therapist can vary considerably. The lowest-paid 10 percent of massage therapists make less than $20,000 a year, while the highest-paid 10 percent earn more than $69,000 each year. That is a gap of almost $50,000! Some of the most well paid can make over $100,000, but this is rare.

High-Level Earnings

Some of the most well-paid massage therapists earn over $50,000 a year without ever having gone to college. At the age of thirty-one, Andrea is one of the few. "It was hard getting to this point," Andrea admits. "It would have been easier to stay at my previous job, but I wanted to earn more." This drive to succeed eventually led Andrea to owning her own massage therapy business.

In addition to learning how to run a business, one of the most difficult aspects of Andrea's new venture was finding her own clients. "After working at so many different spas, I knew plenty of people in the business. It was easy enough to find clients to come to me, but it was still a slow process." During the first few years of her business, Andrea was

making even less money than she was at a spa. "I quickly learned how important it is to **network**," Andrea says. By joining professional organizations and speaking with doctors, Andrea became better known in the massage therapy **community**. "Doctors began referring patients directly to me, which helped a lot. I also posted my information online."

Looking at the Words

To **network** is to talk to and connect with people to further your career.

A **community** is a group of people who share something in common.

Even though Andrea was starting to become successful, this success came with a price. After working on her own for a few years, she was eventually booking more appointments than she could handle. "At one point, I was doing massages forty hours a week. That didn't include the time it took me to order supplies and book appointments and clean up between clients. It was too much for me to deal with all by myself," she says. "Sometimes, I felt completely overwhelmed."

Andrea's solution to her problem was to hire an additional massage therapist. "I figured that between the two of us, we could handle all of the work." The added expertise also made Andrea's business more popular. While Andrea now takes care of most rehabilitative and sports massage therapy appointments, her partner handles everything to do with relaxation and stress-relief massage therapy. Together, they can make most clients happy.

Now that her business has been open for five years, Andrea is making about $63,000 a year. Even though her salary is far above average, a massage therapist can still make much more. The highest paid massage therapists can earn over $100,000 each year. "I am aware of how much I could make if I expanded my business even more or moved somewhere else," Andrea says, "but I have no desire to pursue anything more for now. I am happy with where I am, and that's all that matters to me."

Average Salaries

Although Andrea is earning a very high salary, not every massage therapist will make this much. According to the Bureau of Labor Statistics, the average salary for a massage therapist in 2010 was $34,900. Considering you don't need a college education to become a massage therapist, this salary is more than respectable, since the average salary for all occupations within the United States is slightly less at $33,840 per year.

"I began working for a local spa when I was twenty-one," Andrea remembers. "During my first full year, I made about $25,000. It was enough to survive and it was certainly more than I was making at other jobs." At her first job, Andrea was making the average salary of all healthcare support occupations, a group that includes massage therapists.

Because most massage therapists work part time, a full-time massage therapist has the potential to make a lot of money. Unfortunately, even if a massage therapist wants more hours, these extra hours are not always easy to find. "In general, if you work in a more popular location, you'll get more hours," Andrea advises. "In small towns, there usually aren't all that many people who want or can afford a massage. In cities, you'll get more people making appointments."

Before Andrea decided to open her own business, she worked at several different spas. Andrea says, "The first place I worked did not pay well. It was very small, and not many people came through. The tips were small, too." After Andrea gained more experience, she began working at a more popular spa. In addition to better pay and more appointments,

she received higher tips, because the treatments at this spa were more expensive.

Other factors can affect the amount of work a massage therapist gets. For example, if you work at a popular resort hotel, you will have more clients during the busiest vacationing months. "There is certainly a busy season and a slow season in some areas," explains Andrea. "Not all locations experience this, but it is something to consider when deciding where to live. I have a friend who works at a resort in Malibu. She makes a ton of money during the months when all the tourists are there. Then it slows down for her between times."

On her road to success, Andrea took classes and learned about different modalities. She became certified in all areas of massage, including rehabilitative therapy. Being more **versatile** allowed her to offer more services, and it prepared her for owning her own business.

"Learn a lot. Don't be afraid to step out of your comfort zone," Andrea suggests. "Sometimes, the only way you'll be able to earn more is by taking a risk and doing something new."

CHAPTER 5

Looking to the Future

Massage therapy is one occupation that is expanding at a healthy rate. While all occupations in the United States are growing at 14 percent, massage therapy is growing at 20 percent, far above average rate of growth. What all this means is that the field of massage therapy is growing so fast that new massage therapists like Rob Carlos will probably not have a hard time finding work and staying employed.

There are currently over 150,000 licensed massage therapists in the United States alone. By 2020, this number is

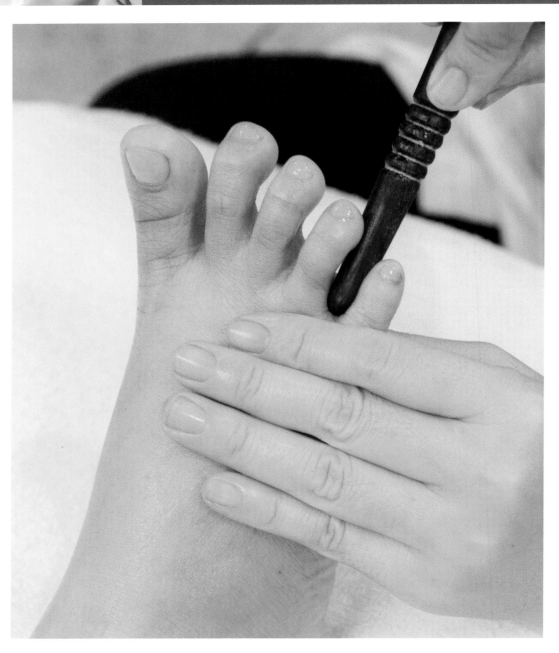

A reflexologist applies pressure with a wooden tool to a patient's foot.

expected to jump to at least 180,000 and possibly even higher. Although most massage therapists are self-employed, others can be found in spas, hotels, doctor offices, and fitness centers. As society's view of massage therapy changes, massage therapists may be found in even more locations. Finding a massage therapist in a business office or nursing home is becoming more common than it once was.

Reflexology

Massage therapists have always believed that massage is directly connected to a body's overall wellness. Today, this belief is more accepted than it once was. Some people are also discovering the benefits of a special type of foot massage known as a reflexology massage. Unlike a massage that might just help the back or neck, a reflexology massage is said to help the body as a whole. Each location on a foot is believed to be connected to a certain body part or organ system. By having each special location on a foot rubbed, it can make the connected areas of the body feel more at ease.

Discoveries and Acceptance

One reason for the expansion of massage therapy as a field is society's increasing acceptance of it. While some people may have doubted the

One career option is to be certified in animal massage. Equissage, a training program for dog and horse massage therapy, says on its website: "The most important qualification for success . . . is a love of animals, empathy for suffering animals, and a sincere desire to help alleviate that suffering. While it would be preferable to have a background in massage therapy, it is not mandatory."

effectiveness of massage therapy in the past, many people now understand the benefits of relaxation massage therapy.

Some companies will even hire massage therapists to visit their offices and offer free massages to employees. "I have been hired to visit a few offices," Rob explains. "The employees like the massages because it helps them deal with all the stress they face on the job." Employers believe these massages help their employees do the best work they can.

Massage therapy has become so accepted that many **insurance companies** will cover the cost of therapy if a doctor recommends it.

Looking at the Words

Insurance companies are businesses that sell insurance, which is financial protection against certain risks such as health problems and damage to homes.

Massages for Pets

Recently, massage therapy has also been used on animals. Even though pets can't tell us directly, they can experience muscle pain just like we do. Some massage therapists are hired to give massages to pets that have muscle pain due to old age or sickness.

Do You Have a Passion?

There's a lot of talk about passion these days: "Find your passion... Pursue your passion... Do what you love..."

Passion, it turns out, lives in all sorts of places. And while finding your passion is an elusive pursuit, there is only one real formula: try things. Try things and see how they fit. Try jobs and find out what you like—and just as important, find out what you don't like.

The most important thing is: Don't feel overwhelmed if you don't have a passion. Don't feel like there's something wrong with you. And then ask yourself: What is something I enjoy doing? What is something I've done already that had aspects to it I liked?

Passion can come later. Right now, just find something you enjoy. That's a starting point. Maybe it'll become that thing you can do for hours and it feels like only a few minutes have gone by. But don't put that pressure on yourself. Start small.

*"Our work is to discover our work
and then with all our heart to give ourselves to it."*
—Buddha

Massage therapy has become so popular that some therapists even work in malls, offering massages to shoppers.

"Sometimes, clients will come to me before they see a chiropractor," Rob says. "That way, their muscles and bones can feel better after an injury."

All licensed massage therapists are taught about human anatomy. As the field becomes more popular, more training may be encouraged or even required. "Training is important," Rob confirms, "especially considering all that we are currently discovering." As we learn more about the body, massage therapists can learn more about how to treat it. Likewise, doctors are understanding more about the benefits of massage and recommending it to more patients.

Another reason for the increased interest in massage therapy is connected to the fact that people are living longer than they once did. Modern medicine has allowed people to live much longer than in the past.

Looking to the Future

Today, it's not uncommon for someone to live until seventy or eighty years old, and many people live well beyond that. Unfortunately, an older body is not as strong as a young body. A gentler type of massage may be used on older patients to relieve pain and help keep the muscles strong. Many massage therapists work in nursing homes and spend their entire career helping the elderly.

Conclusion

Every graduating high school student faces the same question: Should I or shouldn't I go to college? There are plenty of arguments either way. Many careers do require college or an even higher education. Other careers, like massage therapy, do not require a college degree (even though some colleges do offer degrees in massage therapy).

"In the end," Rob says, "it's all about figuring out what's best for you. It's not about getting an easy ride—'cause I promise you, becoming a massage therapist is no easy ride! I think whatever you do in life, you go further if you're excited about what you're doing. When you like getting up in the morning, you work harder. You learn new things. You get better and better at what you do. I plan on making a lot more money before I'm done. But that's not what it's all about for me. For me it's all about doing something I love."

Find Out More

IN BOOKS

Ashley, Martin. *Massage: A Career at Your Fingertips: The Complete Guide to Becoming a Bodywork Professional*. Somers, N.Y.: Enterprise, 2006.

Calvert, Robert Noah. *The History of Massage: An Illustrated Survey from Around the World*. Rochester, Ver.: Healing Arts, 2002.

Salvo, Susan G. *Massage Therapy: Principles and Practice*. St. Louis, Mo.: Saunders Elsevier, 2012.

ON THE INTERNET

Everest College, "What Is a Licensed or Certified Massage Therapist?" massagetherapy.everestcollege.edu/certified-massage-therapist

Massage Therapy Foundation
www.massagetherapyfoundation.org

Salary.com, "Dream Job: Massage Therapist"
www.salary.com/dream-job-massage-therapist

Bibliography

About.com. "10 Most Popular Types of Massage." http://altmedicine.about.com/od/massage/a/massage_types.htm (accessed March 1, 2013).

Massage & Bodywork. "The Future of Massage." http://www.massageandbodywork.com/Articles/2008/JanFeb2008/The-FutureofMassage.html (accessed March 1, 2013).

Massage Education Guide. "History of Massage Therapy." http://www.massage-education.com/history-of-massage-therapy.html (accessed March 1, 2013).

Natural Healers. "How to Become a Massage Therapist." http://www.naturalhealers.com/qa/massagecareers.html (accessed March 1, 2013).

United States Bureau of Labor Statistics. "Occupational Outlook Handbook: Massage Therapists." http://www.bls.gov/ooh/healthcare/massage-therapists.htm (accessed March 1, 2013).

Index

About the Author

Connor Syrewicz is a writer and editor from Binghamton, New York. He was raised on Long Island, has a degree in English, and spends most of his time writing and facilitating other creative projects. His interests include art and philosophy, which he actively incorporates into his writing.

Picture Credits